SUPERHUMAN ENDURANCE

Kelly Doudna

Big Buddy Books
An Imprint of Abdo Publishing
abdobooks.com

abdobooks.com

Published by Abdo Publishing, a division of ABDO, PO Box 398166, Minneapolis, Minnesota 55439.

Printed in the United States of America, North Mankato, Minnesota
102021
012022

Design: Emily O'Malley, Mighty Media, Inc.
Production: Mighty Media, Inc.
Editor: Rebecca Felix
Cover Photographs: Shutterstock Images
Interior Photographs: Atlantic Campaigns, p. 23; Carlos Osorio/AP Images, p. 19; DJANDYW.COM AKA NOBODY/Flickr, p. 27; Lauren Hurley/AP Images, p. 21; Libby Jones, p. 17; Shutterstock Images, pp. 5, 7, 9, 11, 13, 15, 25, 29
Design Elements: Shutterstock Images

Library of Congress Control Number: 2021942773

Publisher's Cataloging-in-Publication Data
Names: Doudna, Kelly, author.
Title: Superhuman endurance / by Kelly Doudna
Description: Minneapolis, Minnesota : Abdo Publishing, 2022 | Series: Superhuman science | Includes online resources and index.
Identifiers: ISBN 9781532197000 (lib. bdg.) | ISBN 9781644947166 (pbk.) | ISBN 9781098219130 (ebook)
Subjects: LCSH: Human physiology--Juvenile literature. | Performance--Juvenile literature. | Motor ability--Juvenile literature. | Endurance, Physical--Juvenile literature. | Super powers--Juvenile literature.
Classification: DDC 599.9--dc23

DON'T TRY THIS AT HOME

Many of the superhuman feats described in this book were overseen by trainers and doctors. Do not attempt to re-create these feats. Doing so could cause injury.

CONTENTS

Superheroes have superpowers. But real men and women also have **amazing** abilities. Some people survive **extreme** conditions and activities. They have superhuman endurance!

Some people train so they can run almost constantly for days in a row! They only stop to sleep and use the bathroom.

WHAT IS ENDURANCE?

Endurance is your body's ability to keep working. Everyone's endurance is different. Maybe you can swim five laps in a pool. Maybe you can run for one hour. Or maybe you can easily handle cold weather!

Muscular endurance is a muscle's ability to exert force repeatedly for a long time.

PUSHING THE LIMITS

The human body can survive a lot. But it has limits! The body requires enough oxygen. Its muscles need rest. The body must also keep its **internal** temperature from rising too high or falling too low. Some people train to push these limits.

Doctors have studied endurance athletes to learn about the body's limits.

MUSCLE & MIND

Many things **affect** endurance. One is how well your heart sends oxygen to muscles. Endurance is also part of being physically fit. Being fit allows you to stay active for longer without tiring.

Physical exercise also benefits the mind! It improves brain performance and memory.

Your **desire** to complete an activity **affects** endurance too. Some people **meditate** to help work toward a goal. Others **visualize** their goal before and while performing feats of endurance.

Meditating before exercise can help you focus on a goal during a workout.

MENTAL ENDURANCE

The mind is a powerful tool for endurance. American athlete Pam Smith says **fatigue** can be **overwhelming**.

Smith is an ultramarathon runner.

ULTRAMARATHONS

Any race longer than 26.2 miles (42.2 km) is called an ultramarathon.

Ultramarathon courses often cover many types of terrain.

To fight **fatigue**, Smith mentally breaks ultramarathons into small parts. She locates **landmarks** every few miles. She focuses on reaching the nearest one. Once past that landmark, Smith focuses on the next one.

In 2014, Smith used this practice while running the 100-mile (161-km) Angeles Crest 100. She ran for 21 hours straight to win the women's race!

Pam Smith began trail running in 1992 and ultramarathon running in 2002.

SWIMMING STUNT

American Jim "the Shark" Dreyer performs endurance feats in water. He often pulls a heavy load as he swims. In 2013, Dreyer swam for 51 hours while towing one-half ton (454 kg) of bricks!

Jim Dreyer's 51-hour swim in 2013 was 22 miles (35 km) long. He pulled the bricks in dinghies.

ROW YOUR BOAT

Water was also the setting for British rower Jasmine Harrison's feat of endurance. She completed the Talisker Whisky Atlantic Challenge race in 2021. Harrison rowed 3,000 miles (4,828 km) across the Atlantic Ocean in 70 days, 3 hours, and 48 minutes!

A trio of athletes sets off on the 2015 Atlantic Challenge. Jasmine Harrison rowed a similar boat solo in 2021.

Harrison averaged 20,000 strokes per day during her row. She often rowed for 12 hours straight before taking a break! Harrison was 21 years old when she completed the Atlantic Challenge. That made her the youngest woman ever to row **solo** across an ocean.

Harrison rows across the Atlantic. Her boat was 23 feet (7 m) long.

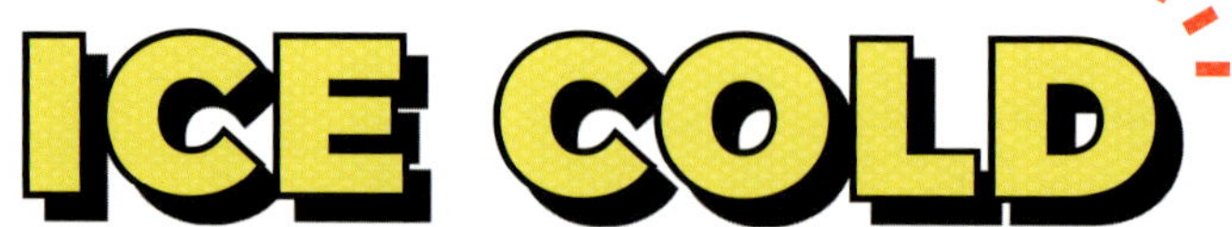

ICE COLD

Some people train to endure **extreme** temperatures. Humans' average body temperature is 98.6 degrees Fahrenheit (37°C). **Hypothermia** sets in if this drops to 95°F (35°C). This can lead to death.

TOO HOT

The hottest **internal** temperature the average human can survive is 108°F (42°C).

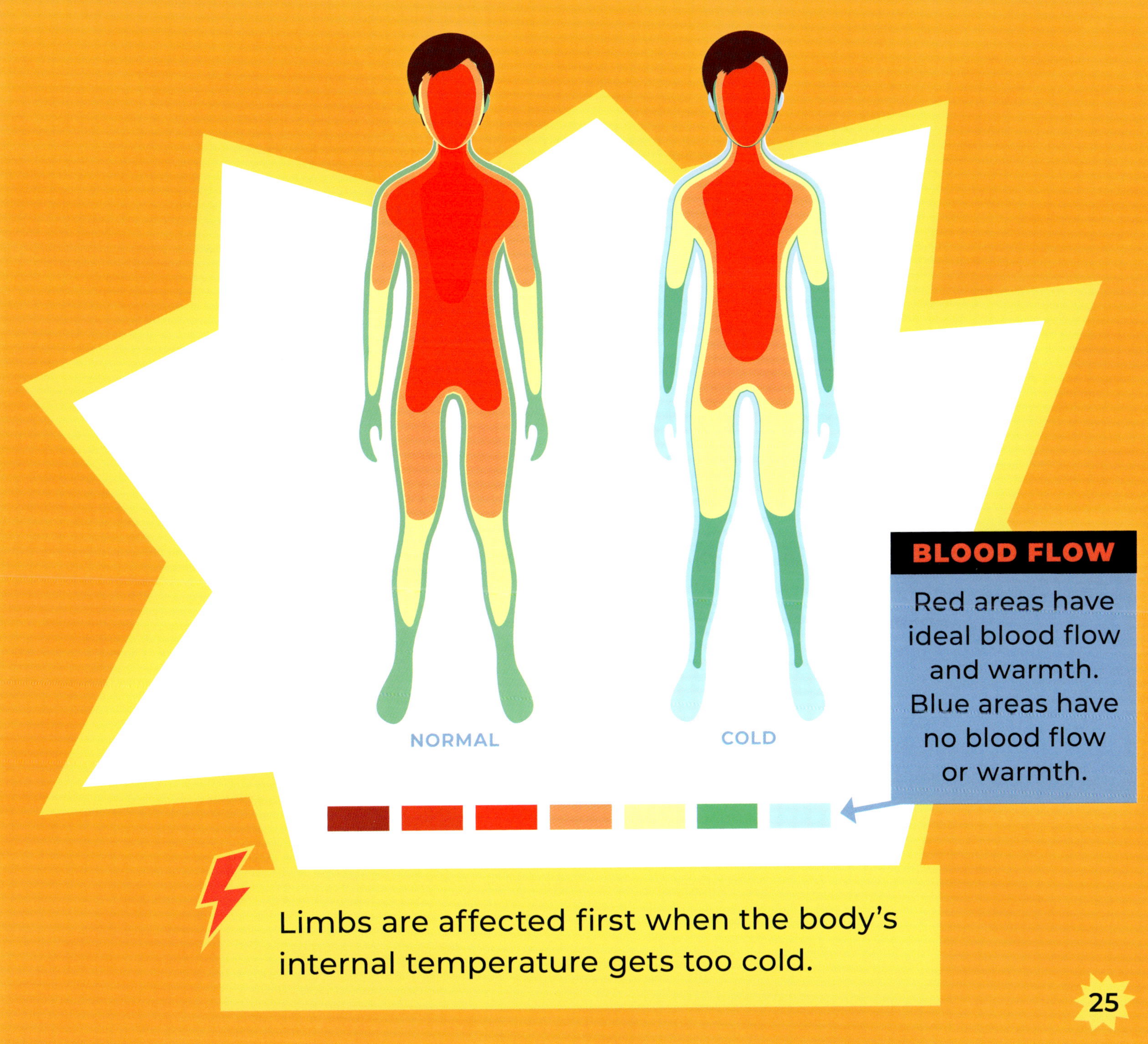

Limbs are affected first when the body's internal temperature gets too cold.

Dutchman Wim Hof is known as "the Iceman." He can survive **encased** in ice for one hour! Hof spent years training his mind and body to endure cold. He uses breathing practices to control his **stress** reaction. He calms his mind using practices from **meditation**.

Wim Hof endures an ice bath wearing devices to monitor his health.

JUMP TO IT

Want to improve your own endurance? Practice jumping!

- Jump rope or do jumping jacks every other day for 30 days.
- On the first day, count how many times you can jump.

- Each day you practice, add a few more jumps. Count each one! Jump until you are tired.

Your endurance will increase quickly! How many jumps can you do by day 30?

GLOSSARY

affect—to cause a change in.

amazing—causing wonder or surprise.

desire—a strong wish or want.

encased—covered in or surrounded by.

extreme (ihk-STREEM)—far beyond the usual.

fatigue—a state of being very tired.

hypothermia—a condition where the body gets so cold that it cannot warm itself again. This slows function in the body and can lead to death.

internal—inside.

landmark—an important building or place.

meditate—to practice the act of thinking deeply and quietly. This practice is called meditation.

overwhelming—causing excess feelings of worry, grief, or another strong emotion.

solo—done alone, by one person.

stress—a feeling of worry that may lead to some illnesses.

visualize—to see or picture mentally.

ONLINE RESOURCES

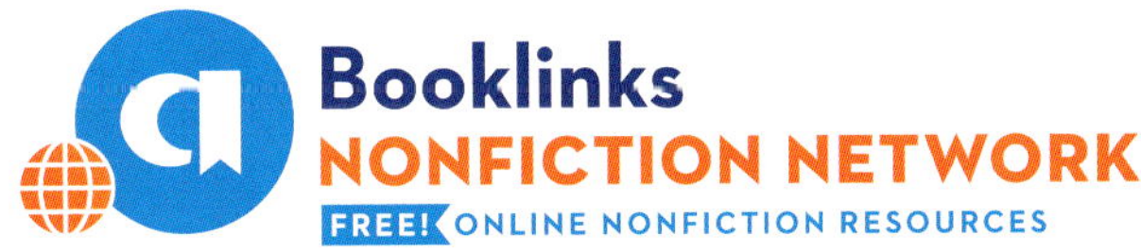

To learn more about superhuman endurance, please visit **abdobooklinks.com** or scan this QR code. These links are routinely monitored and updated to provide the most current information available.

INDEX